# You live in my heart

Alexa Grbic Lash

AuthorHouse™
1663 Liberty Drive
Bloomington, IN 47403
www.authorhouse.com
Phone: 833-262-8899

Because of the dynamic nature of the Internet, any web addresses or links contained in this book may have changed since publication and may no longer be valid. The views expressed in this work are solely those of the author and do not necessarily reflect the views of the publisher, and the publisher hereby disclaims any responsibility for them.

Any people depicted in stock imagery provided by Getty Images are models, and such images are being used for illustrative purposes only. Certain stock imagery © Getty Images.

This book is printed on acid-free paper.

ISBN: 978-1-6655-5389-6(sc)
ISBN: 978-1-6655-5390-2 (e)

Print information available on the last page.

Published by AuthorHouse  03/07/2022

**author**HOUSE®

For Momma, Dad, Chase, Grammy and Abuelo

Yesterday you were here

4

*but today you're gone*

I really miss you and want to see you,
but I can't find you

They told me I couldn't ever see you again but
that you went to a better place

I still don't understand

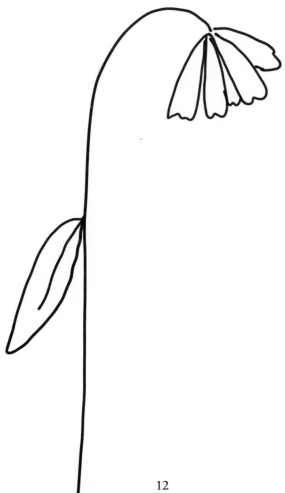

I feel so sad

Then they told me you will ALWAYS be with me because you live in my heart now! That made me feel happy

They also said that my heart is filled with the most beautiful flowers I could ever imagine... and that you feel happy, too!

I know I won't stop missing you...but every time I do,
I can just touch my heart and feel your love.
You will be with me forever.

Printed in the United States
by Baker & Taylor Publisher Services